ONE MINUTE OF *Your* TIME
...RIGHT FROM MY HEART

♥ ♥ ♥

by
Bryant Wright

Published by *RIGHT FROM THE HEART MINISTRIES.*

Manufactured in the United States
First Edition/First Printing

ISBN 0-9660935-0-X

Library of Congress Catalog Number: 97-75425

This book is dedicated to my wife, Anne,

who is my best friend and has given me more love

and respect than any husband deserves.

♥   ♥   ♥

*M*ay I take one minute of your time to thank a few people who helped bring this book into reality...

- Claudia Breed and Philip Self, who provided many original ideas and thoughts that wound up being a part of this effort...

- Deborah Riddle, for providing continual assistance in so many aspects of *RIGHT FROM THE HEART MINISTRIES*...

- Laura Price and Sharon Hosea, for typing and organizing the manuscripts...

- Jerry Maxfield, for giving many hours of selfless devotion in making this book come about. Without him, it would have never happened...

- my Administrative Assistant, Jill Warbington, who keeps my life organized on a daily basis and provided assistance in so many aspects of this project...

- the *RIGHT FROM THE HEART MINISTRIES* Board: John Bovis, Bill Bechtel and Jane Warren, who believed in this project...

- my faithful prayer partners, Randy Pope, Michael Youssef and Andy Stanley, who have all given me great counsel and encouragement...

- the radio listeners and supporters of *RIGHT FROM THE HEART MINISTRIES* whose encouragement made me realize a need for a book like this...

- and finally, the many great folks of Johnson Ferry Baptist Church, who believe in *RIGHT FROM THE HEART MINISTRIES*, and who continually make me thankful that God called me to leave the business world and become a pastor.

Thank you, one and all.

Table of Contents

All scripture references are taken
from the New International and
New American Standard translations.

Section 4

ONE MINUTE FOR OTHERS

Section 5

ONE MINUTE FOR GOD

One Minute of Introduction

Several years ago, Billy Crystal and Jack Palance starred in a fun movie called *CITY SLICKERS*. It was a flick about three good friends at mid-life... taking a break from their demanding corporate jobs to take part in a cattle drive out West. Billy Crystal played the leading role of one of the city slickers, Mitch Robbins, getting away from it all to fulfill a fantasy of being a cowboy for a few weeks. Jack Palance portrayed a hardened cowboy named Curly who was going to show these city slickers a thing or two.

One day Curly asked Mitch if he knew what the secret of life was. Mitch replied, "No, what?" Curly said, "This one thing — just one thing." Mitch asked, "That's great, but what's the one thing?" Curly replied, "That's what you've got to figure out."

Curly was on to something, for there is no doubt in my mind that the meaning of life does come down to "one thing" and *ONE MINUTE OF YOUR TIME* is a collection of thoughts and admonitions written to help you discover what that "one thing" is.

Knowing how busy life is, each idea is designed to take just one minute of your time; but, hopefully these thoughts will stay on your mind much longer than that. If it helps you discover that "one thing", it will have accomplished its purpose. I truly hope it will.

If you find it, you've discovered the answer to life. You accept it and your life will take on fresh meaning and purpose. You receive it and your life will never be the same.

♥ ♥ ♥

ONE MINUTE FOR

~~S~~UCCESSFUL LIVING

*"Do not let
this Book of
the Law depart
from your mouth;
meditate on it day
and night, so that
you may be care-
ful to do every-
thing written in
it. Then you
will be prosperous
and successful."*

JOSHUA 1:8

Do you ever struggle with making the most of your time? Feeling like there's just not enough time in each day? Well, we have to remember we all have the same amount of time: one hundred sixty-eight hours a week, twenty-four hours a day. The key is in making the most of our time. This is a spiritual, as well as practical, issue.

Scripture says, "Be careful, then, how you live, not as unwise men, but as wise, making the most of your time." So what's the key?

1. List the top three to five priorities of your life. This list helps you to prioritize how you spend your time.

2. As you approach each day, write down the

MAKING THE MOST OF YOUR TIME

most important thing you need to do, commit to do it, and then go to the second most important thing and do it. Concentrate on what's most important; major on the majors.

Effective time management is an important discipline to have in order to live the successful life, so get with it before your time runs out.

> "Be careful, then, how you live – not as unwise men, but as wise, making the most of your time."
>
> EPHESIANS 5:15

> "*I seek you with all my heart; do not let me stray from your commands.*"
>
> PSALM 119:10

KEEP YOUR EYES ON THE GOAL

One day a father, walking through freshly fallen snow, wanted to teach his son a key lesson in life. He said, "Son, I'm going to walk to that tree fifty feet ahead in a perfectly straight line. Then I want you to do the same."

The father walked to the tree. He turned to look at his son as they both observed the perfectly straight tracks in the snow. Then the son, looking at his father and not wanting to fail the test, began to walk. He looked down at his steps and veered to the left. He looked up and corrected his course. He looked down again. He veered to the right and had to correct his course once more. Arriving at the tree, his tracks told the story of his failure.

His father explained, "Son, as long as you focused on me, your tracks were straight. The moment you took your eyes off me, you got off track. The key is keeping your eyes on the goal."

So it is in life. There is one primary goal, and if it becomes the heart and focus of our life, it will be the key to eternal success. That goal is following the Lord. Keep your eyes on Him, and He will keep you right on track to where you need to go.

Do you see work as a calling or curse? Is your only reason for working to make a living, or do you live for your work? Is your work drudgery or fulfilling, monotonous or challenging? One thing is certain, it was never meant by God to be a curse. He invented it.

When man was placed in the garden at the beginning of time, God told him to care for it and cultivate it. Obviously that called for work. After man sinned, He said work would be harder, but He still meant it for good.

So how can we have a healthy view of work? Listen to the words of Scripture, "Whatever you do, work at it with all your heart, as working for the Lord, not for men." When we adopt that view, no matter how difficult, no matter how monotonous or challenging, our motivation for work changes. To work heartily to please God is the key to finding meaning in work.

So whatever you do, be it a plumber or a President, a carpenter or a teacher, a janitor or CEO, see your work as a calling and a privilege to serve God by doing your best.

♥   ♥   ♥

WORK ~ A CALLING OR A CURSE?

"Whatever you do, work at it with all your heart, as working for the Lord, not for men..."
COLOSSIANS 3:23

> *"Six days you shall labor and do all your work, but the seventh day is a Sabbath to the Lord your God. On it you shall not do any work . . . For in six days the Lord made the heavens and the earth . . . but he rested on the seventh day."*
>
> EXODUS 20: 9,10A, 11

All of us want to be successful when it comes to our work, but let's think a moment

LAZINESS VS. WORKAHOLISM ~ FINDING THE RIGHT BALANCE

about the two most common problems when it comes to work.

One is laziness. We live in a society that so often glorifies the irresponsible, who won't work, as victims. This is insulting to those who are truly unable to work. God's Word is clear; laziness is not good. God wants us to work hard.

At the other extreme is workaholism, and there are four common traits of the workaholic:

1. He tends to be the person who is the first at the office and the last to leave.

2. Trying to please others, he has a tough time saying no.

3. He tends to only talk about work.

4. He feels guilty in taking a day off. This extreme is not good either.

The right balance is working hard to please God yet taking time to back away and rest. Take a weekly Sabbath— one of God's great ideas for successful living. When we do, we find ourselves refreshed and ready to give our best to our work.

*I*f you could define one common denominator for leaders, what would it be?

1. Obviously, leaders make things happen; they bring about change.

2. Real leaders communicate clearly what they stand for — what their goals are. They have clear direction.

3. Leaders have an ability to motivate others to do what they want them to do. People WANT to follow them. Sometimes this is for good — sometimes it is for evil.

4. Real leaders delegate. They trust in others to get the job done. Micromanagers consistently destroy the morale of those they are called to lead.

All these are key traits of leadership, but what separates leaders from great leaders? I believe that it is COURAGE. The courage to do

LEADERS ARE COURAGEOUS

what is right — to do what needs to be done — especially when the heat is on... and the people are grumbling... and times are hard. Great leaders have the courage to lead others to carry out their vision no matter how hard the course. This courage can be found in the Lord.

Leaders, God's Word says, "Be strong and courageous." Courage is the key in all great leaders.

> *"Have I not commended you? Be strong and courageous. Do not be terrified; do not be discouraged, for the Lord your God will be with you wherever you go."*
> JOSHUA 1:9

♥   ♥   ♥

> *"No one can serve two masters. Either he will hate the one and love the other, or he will be devoted to the one and despise the other. You cannot serve both God and money."*
>
> JESUS CHRIST
> MATTHEW 6:24

THE STOCK MARKET

Are you bullish or bearish? Is the Federal Reserve on the right track or not? When you think about the Dow Jones, is it buy or sell? Hold or liquidate?

As important as financial advice from Wall Street is, there's a more reliable place to gain understanding on managing our money. That place is the Bible. Amazingly, Jesus speaks more about money and possessions than He does about heaven or hell.

The problem is we don't want to do it God's way. God's way says to give, share and provide for those who have less. It's advice diametrically opposed to what our human reason tells us: to get, to keep, to hoard. God's way is to spend less than we earn. The world's way is to charge it. Build up that debt.

Face it. The best financial planner is the Creator of the world. Why not learn what He has to say about managing money and then try it His way.

*A*re you on the road to financial security? Let me suggest a few goals to strive for in seeking personal financial security.

1. You need to know what you make, and if you're on commission, estimate conservatively what it'll be.

2. Spend less than you earn. I know it seems so obvious, but it's so overlooked that it has to be mentioned.

3. Have a personal or family budget. Budgets help us prioritize and meet our goals.

4. In developing that budget, focus on five major categories: 1) a goal for giving; 2) an estimated amount for taxes; 3) a goal for savings and investments; 4) figure up your fixed expenses, such as car, house, groceries, etc.

Finally, what's left is discretionary income and you will want to set goals in this area. It includes such items as clothing, furniture, vacation and entertainment.

From where does all this practical insight come? It's based on

FINANCIAL SECURITY

"How blessed is the man who finds wisdom, and the man who gains understanding."
PROVERBS 3:13

principles right out of the Bible. You'll be amazed that, when you look to Scripture, you'll find the keys to financial security.

♥   ♥   ♥

> *"Remember this:*
> *Whoever sows sparing-*
> *ly will*
> *also reap*

MONEY

> *sparingly, and whoever*
> *sows generously will*
> *also reap generously.*
> *Each man should give*
> *what he has decided in*
> *his heart to give, not*
> *reluctantly or under*
> *compulsion, for God*
> *loves a cheerful giver."*
>
> II CORINTHIANS 9:6-7

In the book, "*DAYS OF GRACE*," Arthur Ashe shares his philosophy about money. He says, "From what we get, we can make a living; what we give, however, makes a life." What a great perspective on money. The focus on giving rather than on getting makes all the difference.

You see, as long as our focus is getting all we can, canning all we get, and sitting on the can — we're a slave to our money. Our happiness depends on how much we have on our financial statement. On the other hand, when we view money as a tool for accomplishing good, then it becomes our servant. That attitude frees us to use money as God intended—to provide not only for our needs, but also to do good for others.

How about it? Are you the master of your money, or the slave to your possessions and your money? A giver or getter? Want to really live? Start to give.

♥   ♥   ♥

People today live pressure-filled lives and it's taking its toll. Dr. Joel Elkes says, "Our mode of life — the way we live — is emerging as today's main cause of illness." The American Academy of Family Physicians states that "1) two-thirds of all visits to doctors are stress related, and 2) stress is now known as the major contributor to heart disease, cancer, accidental injuries and suicide."

People attend stress seminars and devour books on stress. Sometimes they find that just focusing on it makes them more uptight. But let's face it, stress and pressure are a part of life.

Even Jesus Christ promised us that we'll all face it. He said, "In this world you'll face much TRIBULATION." Tribulation also means PRESSURE. He goes on to say, "but take heart. I have overcome the world." Jesus does not promise us freedom from pressure, but He does promise us peace amidst the stress. Inner peace is a by-product of knowing Christ as Savior and Lord. The Good News is it's available to all who trust in Him.

Yes, pressure is a part of life,

PRESSURE

"Peace I leave with you; my peace I give you. I do not give to you as the world gives. Do not let your hearts be troubled and do not be afraid."

JESUS CHRIST
JOHN 14: 27

but Christ gives us peace amidst the pressure... and that's not a bad way to live!

♥   ♥   ♥

The Ten Commandments
EXODUS 20

THE RIGHT VALUES

There's a lot of talk this day and age about values — family values, traditional values, etc. NEWSWEEK ran a cover entitled, "Whose Values?" Well, let me offer a suggestion; it's very old but very contemporary. How about the values that come from man's Creator — from God Himself?

They go like this:

"You shall have no other gods before Me.

You shall not make for yourself an idol.

You shall not take the name of the Lord your God in vain.

Remember the Sabbath Day.

Honor your father and mother.

You shall not murder.

You shall not commit adultery.

You shall not steal.

You shall not bear false witness.

You shall not covet."

These are not suggestions to be used when you feel they are appropriate; they are absolute; how to live life to the fullest.

Whose values? I encourage you to adopt God's Big Ten. You'll find that they will be a key to living life to the fullest.

*L*et's talk about temptation. How do you keep that decision to do wrong from getting the best of you?

Realize that temptation is just a part of life. The Bible tells us Jesus was tempted in every way we are— EVERY WAY. The big difference in Him and all of us is that He never gave in to it.

So how can we keep temptation from getting the best of us?

1. Just say NO — Don't take time to flirt with it, or even argue. JUST SAY NO.

2. Then scram — get out of there! This is one time in life when running is not cowardly but the bravest thing you can do.

3. Ask God's help resisting it... for those too tough to resist... those you battle constantly. Simply admit they are too tough and ask God's help in resisting them. The power of the only Man never to give in to temptation is available to all of us, if we'll just confess our weakness and admit our need for Him and His strength.

Overcoming temptation is a key to successful living.

♥   ♥   ♥

VICTORY OVER TEMPTATION

"No temptation has seized you except what is common to man. And God is faithful; He will not let you be tempted beyond what you can bear. But when you are tempted, He will also provide a way out so that you can stand up under it."

I CORINTHIANS 10: 13

Jesus Walks on Water
MATTHEW 14:22-33

OVERCOMING FEAR

To learn courage you have to know fear. Isaac Stern, the great violinist, observing a nine year old playing the violin amazingly, remarked this way, "You can't really tell how an artist will be until the teen years, for that is when fear comes in. Then and only then can you see if the person has courage. You can't learn courage until you know fear."

Fear can paralyze us. Finding the courage to overcome it is a real key to successful living. One day Jesus' disciples were caught at sea in a storm. They were afraid they wouldn't make it. Jesus walked out to them and said, "Take courage! It is I. Do not be afraid."

That's the key to finding courage in the face of fear. It comes through faith in Jesus Christ. Fear and faith do not mix — they're like oil and water. You see when faith kicks in, fear moves out, and when faith disappears, fear moves in like a tidal wave. The key to finding the courage to overcome fear is faith.

There's an Arab proverb that goes like this: "All sunshine makes for a desert." Have you ever thought of life that way? All of us want things to go our way all the time, but we have to admit that life just doesn't work like that. Hard times come; relationships are damaged and even destroyed; financial worries plague us. Yes, the clouds and the storms really do come.

Jesus said, "In this world you will have trouble." But the good news is that He didn't stop there. He also said, "But take heart. I have overcome the world." Yes, trouble is a fact of life. Jesus Christ has given us a means of finding a victory — the real victory, even in hard times. Won't you allow Him to provide all you need to face the good times and the bad? He's willing and able to provide the victory — even when things look the darkest.

❤   ❤   ❤

> **TRIALS**
>
> "And we know that in all things God works for the good of those who love Him, who have been called according to His purpose."
>
> ROMANS 8:28

> *"Who shall separate us from the love of Christ? Shall trouble or hardship or persecution or famine or nakedness or danger or sword... No, in all these things we are more than conquerors through Him who loved us."*
>
> ROMANS 8: 35, 37

WINNING THE RACE

During the filming of the old classic movie, *BEN HUR*, Charlton Heston had a terrible time learning to drive the chariot. As the time for the filming of the key sequence of the chariot race drew near, Heston told the director, "I think I can drive the chariot, but I don't think I can win the race." The director replied, "You just drive, and I'll see to it that you win."

Wouldn't it be great if we could be assured of victory in life? Wouldn't you like to know that, even though the circumstances don't always seem to be in our favor, the ultimate outcome would be positive?

I've got good news for you. This principle does hold true. Those who place their trust in Jesus Christ, who seek to follow His guidance and direction for living, can be sure of ultimate victory through eternal life. Live life God's way — He assures the victory.

Have you ever noticed window washers at work on a sky scraper? Why do you suppose they can work so confidently suspended so high above the ground? They are secure because they have faith that their safety harnesses will hold even if the platform should fall.

Your life can be lived on the edge with confidence like that. When we give our lives to Jesus Christ, He becomes our safety and security. Because of Him, we can risk living life to the fullest in the process — be all that we were created to be. Because our faith is in Him, He keeps us secure, even though life itself is often insecure — especially when we meet disappointment and the bottom falls out.

How about you? Do you have security for today — no matter what challenges and dangers you face? How about tomorrow? Why not try living life with Christ — a life that is secure and full of excitement — because living life in faith is the ultimate way to live life on the edge.

♥ ♥ ♥

LIVING ON THE EDGE

"For I am convinced that neither death nor life, neither angels nor demons, neither the present nor the future, nor any powers, neither height nor depth, nor anything else in all creation, will be able to separate us from the love of God that is in Christ Jesus our Lord."

ROMANS 8: 38-39

Yourself

"...I say to every man among you not to think more highly of himself than he ought to think; but to think so as to have sound judgement..."

ROMANS 12:3

One of the rarest commodities in society is contentment. Advertisers would have us believe that their product is the key to finding fulfillment and happiness. Television programming reinforces this message and fills our homes with images of things. It's like this bunch of "stuff" is essential to our happiness. Seeking satisfaction in things will never bring about contentment. As a matter of fact, it just leads to further dissatisfaction.

So how do we find contentment? Like so many other things, contentment is a choice — a by-product. A man who had more than his share of difficulty in life said, "I have learned to be content regardless of my circumstances." That was the apostle Paul. How did he do it? The key was found in his relationship with Jesus Christ. That's the key for anyone. We all have the same opportunity to find contentment. It's a by-product of our relationship with Jesus Christ, our Savior and Lord. That is the key to being content.

CONTENTMENT

♥   ♥   ♥

"I am not saying this because I am in need, for I have learned to be content whatever the circumstances."

THE APOSTLE PAUL
PHILIPPIANS 4:1 1

> *"In the morning, O Lord, you hear my voice; in the morning I lay my requests before you and wait in expectation."*
>
> PSALM 5:3

GETTING OFF TO A GOOD START IN THE MORNING

Are you a morning person or a night person? Millions of people don't get going until about three o'clock in the afternoon. That's when their creative juices start flowing and when they really feel alive. For most of us, that's a down time and the day begins much earlier. Because of commitments to work and school, my wife and I have to be up and going in the morning. Even if you're a night owl, let me suggest a great way to start your day. The writer of Psalms knew the key: "In the morning, O Lord, You will hear my voice (or prayer)."

Doesn't it make sense to be in touch with the One who created the day in the first place? Why not begin with a few minutes alone with God each morning. Study God's Word and share with Him your heart and your concerns through prayer. It helps get you in the right frame of mind. You'll find your day will start, and finish, a whole lot better.

Some feel it in a crowd; others feel it when alone. Sociologists say that never before in history have so many people lived so close together and felt so far apart. Loneliness is a major problem of our age. There is no doubt that singles bars are filled with people battling loneliness. A divorced person, tired of one-night stands, recently said: "Sex is readily available in the American singles scenes, but friendship is not."

I propose to you that one can still be alone but not lonely. As a matter of fact, a person will never find victory over loneliness until they learn to enjoy being alone. You see, at the root of all loneliness is alienation from God.

ALONE, BUT NOT LONELY

Years ago, a man named Augustine espoused that God has made us for Himself. Our soul is restless until we find rest in Him. We may seek to fill the void of a restless soul with activities, crowds and noise, but a nagging loneliness will always be there until a we have a personal relationship with God. When we find that, we will have found the key to being alone, but not lonely.

♥   ♥   ♥

> "...I am with you always, to the very end of the age."
>
> JESUS CHRIST
> MATTHEW 28: 20

> *"If you forgive men for their transgressions, your heavenly Father will also forgive you."*
>
> JESUS CHRIST
> MATTHEW 6:14

FORGIVENESS

Do you sometimes struggle with feelings of bitterness and resentment? Perhaps when that person at work gets a promotion that you feel like you deserved, or when a friend or spouse betrays you.

Let me tell you about a person who had every reason to be bitter. He was accused of being a trouble-maker and He only told the truth. One of His closest aides betrayed Him and turned Him in to the authorities. At His trial, people made up lies about Him.

He was beaten by the prison guards. He was sentenced to death by a judge responding to a lynch mob. While He was being executed and people were making fun of Him, He prayed, "Father, forgive them, for they don't know what they're doing." I'm talking about Jesus Christ, the Person who had every reason to feel bitter, but who chose to forgive.

Let Jesus Christ be your model to follow. Ask God to help you forgive that person who has wronged you and you'll feel free at last.

Dr. Michael DeBakey, the famous heart surgeon, once received a letter from an 11-year-old girl with this question, "Is there any love in an artificial heart?" Love is illusive, yet we all long for it.

How would you define love? Most everyone knows it is real, but who can really describe it? I can't define love, but God's Word sure can. The Bible says, "Love is patient and kind, not envious or selfish or arrogant. Love doesn't keep records when people let us down or do us wrong. Love forgives. Love is happy for others' successes. Love is very optimistic. Love bears all things. It believes in others and what they can be, thus putting up with a lot. Love hopes for the best in others. True love never gives up, it just keeps on keeping on. It means a commitment to love a person whether they love us or not.

Is love found in an artificial heart? I'm afraid not, but love can be found in an old heart made new by the power of the Great Physician, Jesus Christ.

♥   ♥   ♥

WHAT LOVE IS

"*This is how we know what love is: Jesus Christ laid down his life for us. And we ought to lay down our lives for our brothers.*"

1 JOHN 3:16

> *"And the peace of God, which surpasses all comprehension, shall guard your hearts and your minds in Christ Jesus."*
>
> PHILIPPIANS 4:7

PEACE IN A PLANE CRASH

We were dropping out of the sky... five of us on a twin engine Cessna. The right engine had gone out and then the left. We knew within a minute or two we would crash. A lot of thoughts went through my head. My wife and I had a three-month-old son. Would he grow up without a father? I prayed that God would guide the pilot in bringing us down. Amazingly, in a way I can't explain, a peace came over me. It was a sureness that we would be okay, whether we lived or died, because all of us knew Christ.

We crashed in a rice field. Part of the left wing broke off. We belly-flopped down, spun to a stop, and all walked away unharmed. Yes, it was a miracle, but even more, to be face to face with death and not be afraid — that meant everything. If you were in my seat, how would you have felt? The Good News is that with Jesus Christ we can face death knowing God's victory.

*D*o you need a good dose of joy? It really is good medicine. Years ago, PSYCHOLOGY TODAY magazine carried an article, "Laugh and Be Well," in which Norman Cousin wrote about his remarkable recovery from a disabling condition through massive doses of Vitamin C and comedy clips. His experience spawned a new field of scientific research on the way in which the brain influences the immune system. The Bible has said it all along.

In Proverbs, God's Word says, "A cheerful heart is good medicine, but a crushed spirit dries up the bones." Do you need a good dose of joy, yet nothing seems to ease the pain? I have good news - you can find joy. It is found in a Person who is the source of a lasting joy that overcomes the heartaches of life. His name is Jesus. Jesus says, "I've told you these things, that My joy may be in you, and that your joy may be made full."

We all need to enjoy laughter. It's good medicine, but lasting joy is only found in Jesus.

> *"A cheerful heart is good medicine, but a crushed* JOY *spirit dries up the bones."*
> PROVERBS 17:22

> *"Patience of spirit is better than haughtiness of spirit."*
>
> **PATIENCE**
>
> ECCLESIASTES 7:8

*I*t has been said that life is a test in patience. Where do you struggle with being patient? I struggle with lines, whether it's traffic or waiting at a restaurant. I'd rather drive five miles out of the way than sit still in traffic. I get impatient with people when I'm facing a deadline and get interrupted or when people tell me they'll do something and it doesn't get done.

Where do you struggle with patience? Do you ever pray, "Lord, give me some patience — NOW!" Let me suggest a few practical ways to learn patience:

1. Take a breath and pray for self-control.

2. If possible, when people anger you, retreat a moment. Take time to back off and get control of your emotions.

3. Confront fairly and seek to listen, understand, and where needed, to forgive.

4. Remember, the greatest motive for patience is remembering God's patience with us.

Patience is a precious commodity, for it is a powerful way to win the respect of others and turn a potential enemy into a friend.

Do you know one character trait that is always appreciated? The Biblical proverb tells us: "What is desirable in a man is his kindness."

In the movie *THE FUGITIVE*, it was the acts of kindness done by the character played by Harrison Ford that caused the cop obsessed with chasing him to question whether this fugitive could have really killed his wife. When the fugitive risked his own cover to save the life of a boy who was being neglected in a busy hospital emergency room, you could just see the cop thinking: "Cold-blooded killers don't do things like this."

Acts of kindness inspire us; whether it's taking time to help out a new employee at the office, a child helping an elderly neighbor, or someone who defends a weaker person picked on by bullies. Are you known by selfless acts of kindness?

♥   ♥   ♥

> "...*Put on a heart of compassion...and kindness...*"
>
> ## KINDNESS
>
> COLOSSIANS 3:12

> *"Do you not know that those who run in a race all run, but only one receives the prize? Run in such a way that you may win."*
>
> I CORINTHIANS 9:24

SELF-CONTROL

Do you ever say, "It was just too tempting," or "I wish I hadn't lost my cool"? A real key to successful living is self-control, that is, controlling our emotions, desires, passions or tongue. In short, self-control is about self-discipline.

The Bible compares it to sports. In a race, everyone runs, but only one person gets first prize. Run your race to win. The Bible says: "Everyone who competes in the games exercises self-control in all things." Self-control is essential to success in living as well as in sports.

So let me suggest a few ways to learn it:

1. CLARIFY YOUR PURPOSE: What are you trying to accomplish? If your goal is to win an Olympic medal, the decisions you make will be shaped by that purpose.

2. BE HONEST WITH YOURSELF: Where do you lack self-control? Alcoholics who find victory over booze know the first step is admitting their inability to control the problem.

3. ASK GOD FOR SELF-CONTROL: He can provide the necessary strength in areas where you lack self-control.

4. TAKE ACTION ON THAT DISCIPLINE: Don't think it will come automatically. Take it one day at a time.

♥　　♥　　♥

*L*osing a loved one or close friend is never easy. If you have recently faced the death of someone you love, or know someone who has, understanding the stages of grief can help.

Grief involves:

1. NUMBNESS — an inability to feel when the news of death arrives.

2. DENIAL — a sense of disbelief that the person is really gone.

3. TEARFUL EMOTION — as the reality of permanent separation sets in.

4. ANGER — at God or life itself as the world continues on, when you are hurting so badly.

5. DEPRESSION — in feeling there is little reason to live. Life may seem meaningless when the loss of a loved one has occurred.

6. ACCEPTANCE — coming to terms with the loss and beginning to move on.

GETTING THROUGH GRIEF

The grieving process takes time — sometimes months and sometimes years — but it can be overcome. The greatest strength for getting through it can be found in the Lord. Remember, God understands grief. He knows what it's like to have a child die. He saw His own Son, Jesus, die for us all. He loves you and wants to help you overcome your grief. Just tell Him you need His help.

♥   ♥   ♥

> *"Blessed are those who mourn, for they shall be comforted."*
>
> JESUS CHRIST
> MATTHEW 5:4

> *"Be strong, and let your heart take courage, all you who hope in the Lord."*
> PSALM 31:24

COURAGE

On June 6, 1994, the world observed the fiftieth anniversary of the allied landing at Normandy. It was a day of overwhelming tragedy and innumerable acts of courage. When hearing the accounts of bravery performed on those beaches, I was absolutely awed by those men who distinguished themselves in fighting for freedom.

Acts of courage don't occur only on the battlefield. Courageous deeds happen unnoticed on the playground, in offices, and in homes every day as people stand up for what is right. Courage is understanding the risk and choosing to do the right thing anyway.

Two thousand years ago, a man named Jesus Christ, who had never sinned, chose to go to the cross for your sins and for mine. It was the ultimate act of courage. His sacrifice, like that of the men at Normandy, was for you. When you finally recognize what His sacrifice means, I encourage you to choose to trust Him. When you do, you will find the eternal freedom that was won for you through His courage.

The idea that the pace of life seems to continually increase stress and worry is a universal concept. There seems to be no end to the demands on our time and energy. Are you tired of the rat race?

There is a solution; not one which offers escape from the demands of life, but one which guarantees REST in the midst of the rat race and the fast pace of life. Jesus says, "Come to ME if you are tired and burdened. I'll make your load lighter, and help you carry your burden." Jesus offers us rest amidst the stress.

Christ doesn't always take us OUT of life's

REST FOR THE WEARY

demanding situations. Instead, He invites us to allow Him to help us handle the demands. He wants to face each day and each challenge with us. Walking with Jesus Christ daily and trusting Him for guidance and wisdom to handle whatever comes is the way to experience REST in the rat race.

♥   ♥   ♥

"Take my yoke upon you and learn from me, for I am gentle and humble in heart, and you will find rest for your souls."
JESUS CHRIST
MATTHEW 11:29

> *"I, even I, am He who comforts you."*
> ISAIAH 51:12

TROUBLE

Corporate downsizing... rebellious teenagers... an unfaithful spouse... a devastating illness... life often brings a lot of trouble our way. Sometimes we are overwhelmed and struggle to merely stay afloat.

Difficulty in trouble should come as no surprise to students of the Bible. Jesus Christ said in John 16:33, "In this world you will have problems." Now that doesn't sound like a very optimistic outlook. Then He goes on to say: "But take heart! I have overcome the world." Now, that message is positive indeed.

Trouble... difficulty... they are a reality in this life. Jesus Christ promises us that He has provided victory over those things which cause us so much pain. Trusting in Him is the key to overcoming these problems.

Why not re-evaluate your present struggles from a Biblical perspective... from Christ's perspective? You have nothing to lose and everything to gain! Jesus Christ is the key.

Do you ever wish that certain people got what you felt they deserved? Especially people that have wronged you? People that seem to get away with murder and not face any kind of punishment or repercussion?

You may have seen the cartoon with three panels.

Panel #1: A most zealous character is praying to the Almighty. He says, "God, smite my worst enemy!"

Panel #2: The man praying this prayer is struck by lightning.

Panel #3: The man groggily says, "God, let me rephrase that!"

We have to watch out how we pray, because sometimes we might find out that our own worst enemy is ourselves. Jesus Christ says, "Do not judge lest you be judged. For in the way you judge others you will be judged as well."

I hope that today you won't be so hard on others, because one day, the hammer may fall down on you.

♥   ♥   ♥

REVENGE-THE WRONG WAY TO PRAY

> "Do not judge, or you too will be judged. For in the same way you judge others, you will be judged, and with the measure you use, it will be measured to you."
>
> JESUS CHRIST
> MATTHEW 7:1, 2

> *"Do not be deceived,*
> *God is not mocked; for*
> *whatever*
> *a man*
> *sows, this*
> *he will also reap."*
>
> GALATIANS 6:7

REAPING WHAT YOU SOW

A young teenager wanted to aggravate the hard-working farmer that lived next door. He led some of his pals to sneak into the farmer's field one night and spread crab grass seeds all over the farm. Soon, the crab grass came up. He laughed every time he saw the farmer vainly trying to get rid of it.

A few years later, long after the teenager forgot his prank, he fell in love with the farmer's daughter and soon they were married. When her father died, he inherited the farm and for the rest of his life he battled that sorry crab grass that he had spread all over his fields.

The Bible says, "For whatever a man sows, this he will also reap." In short, when we're hard on others, people tend to be hard on us. When we're kind to others, they tend to be kind to us. It's the law of the harvest. When you plant tomatoes, you don't get squash, for the harvest never lies.

What kind of seeds are you sowing and what kind of harvest are you reaping? Let's remember in life that we reap what we sow.

Everyone has seen the Nike commercial. The implication is that all that is needed to become an athlete is determination, hard work and those shoes. When it comes to human nature, life is very different. Human beings just aren't disciplined enough to do all we need to do. We can't change ourselves by our own initiative.

One of the Biblical writers, an avid sports fan by the name of Paul, recognized that changing human nature calls on something else — a supernatural change agent. Our only responsibility is to be willing to allow that change agent to bring about the needed improvements.

No, He might not improve your golf game, even though I wish He would. He may not give you the ability to hit home runs. He will adjust your attitude, your character and your relationships for the better, however. So, JUST DO IT. Allow Christ to change you from an ineffective, frustrated self-improver to a winner in the game of life.

♥   ♥   ♥

JUST DO IT

"Abide in Me, and I in you. As the branch cannot bear fruit of itself, unless it abides in the vine, so neither can you, unless you abide in Me."

JESUS CHRIST
JOHN 15:4

> *"If someone forces you to go one mile, go with him two miles."*
>
> JESUS CHRIST
> MATTHEW 5:41

THAT SLIGHT EDGE

In 1992, I had the opportunity to attend the Olympics in Barcelona. The swimming competition fascinated me. The difference between the best in the world was so slight. Sometimes just tenths of a second was the difference between winning the gold and not winning any medal. Now that's a slight edge.

Very often the difference between being an "also-ran" and being a champion is simply that "slight edge." Jesus tells us that principle is applicable to being a champion human being. He says, "If someone asks you for your shirt, give him your coat as well. If someone over you orders you to walk one mile, go with him two." That slight edge in helping others and giving extra effort can mean all the difference in the world in being a champion human being.

When it comes to living life, be it accomplishment or character, very often the key to greatness is that simple "slight edge."

♥   ♥   ♥

*I*n the late 70's to early 80's the fitness craze began to sweep America. The number of joggers went from a thousand oddballs to millions dashing across the landscape of America. Even the former communist sympathizer turned consummate capitalist, Jane Fonda, produced her first workout video, and suddenly fitness was really in style.

That's a good thing, for taking care of our bodies is an important spiritual principle. Think about the most common ways people abuse their bodies: smoking... alcohol and drug abuse... lack of regular exercise... and of course, overeating. For years I've seen and heard Baptist preachers railing against the evils of alcohol while standing there so fat and out of shape that they make a hog look petite. What hypocrisy! Gluttony is just as real a sin as drunkenness.

So today, I urge you, make a decision to get in shape and take care of your body. It's an important spiritual discipline.

♥   ♥   ♥

TAKING CARE OF YOUR BODY

> *"Or do you not know that your body is a temple of the Holy Spirit who is in you, whom you have from God, and that you are not your own? For you have been bought with a price; therefore, glorify God in your body."*
>
> I CORINTHIANS 6:19, 20

> *"I am the light of the world; whoever follows Me will never walk in darkness, but will have the light of life."*
>
> JESUS CHRIST
> JOHN 8:12

THE LIGHTHOUSE

Tom Landry tells the story of a battleship seeing the light of another ship coming directly toward it in the middle of the night. The captain of the other ship radioed to the coming ship and said, "Turn south immediately." The response was, "You turn south immediately."

The captain was furious. He radioed back, "This is a battleship. I command you to turn south immediately." The response was, "This is the lighthouse. You turn south immediately."

So often that captain's attitude is like all of us. We are arrogant towards God and mankind. We expect others to get out of our way and we ignore God's guidance for living our life. Suddenly, we find ourselves shipwrecked and feeling like fools.

Jesus Christ is the lighthouse trying to warn us of danger, to lead us to safety. I encourage you to trust Christ and be willing to follow His leadership in your life. He'll keep you out of a lot of trouble.

What's going to happen next year... next week... 15 minutes from now? Many people waste time in the present worrying about the future. The Bible gives us a wonderful promise. God says, "I know the plans I have for you... plans to prosper you and not to harm you, plans to give you a hope and a future."

Can we know the future? No, but we can face the future with confidence when we know that God is in control of it and He is working for our good. No matter what circumstances come our way, we know He is there for us. Frankly, when I read the newspapers, or see the evening news, I don't always feel optimistic about the future. When I keep my focus on God, knowing He is in control, I have hope for tomorrow and am able to enjoy living for today.

♥   ♥   ♥

THE FUTURE

> "'For I know the plans I have for you,' declares the Lord, 'plans to prosper you and not to harm you, plans to give you hope and a future.'"
>
> JEREMIAH 29:11

USE IT OR LOSE IT

I have friends who are learning to speak Spanish. They're struggling with different sounds, different sentence structure, and different words. Acquiring a new skill takes practice and patience. You've heard the cliche, "Use it or lose it." My friends realize that they have to use the few Spanish words they know or they quickly forget them. We must USE what we know, or we don't retain knowledge.

This principle applies in the spiritual dimension as well. Faith in God is like a muscle. The more you use it, the stronger it becomes. The manual for getting the muscle in shape is the Bible and the personal trainer is Jesus Christ. If you submit yourself to His leadership and His guidance, you'll discover how to use the faith muscle each and every day. It's either use it or lose it. I hope that you'll choose to use it. You'll be amazed at how your faith will grow day by day.

♥ ♥ ♥

He was exhausted — completely worn out from dealing with people and their problems. What He needed was a rest. He got away to spend some time alone with God. When He did, His spirit was renewed and refreshed. When the crowds came, He was able to respond — to care for them and meet their needs.

His name was Jesus Christ and He was the busiest man who ever lived. He accomplished more than anyone before or since.

You know, we live in a very fast-paced world with great demands, yet no one has ever been busier than Jesus when He walked on this earth. Why not learn from Him when you're frazzled, exhausted and burned out. Take some time to be with God. If Jesus needed some time alone with God, we surely do as well.

♥   ♥   ♥

THE BUSIEST MAN WHO EVER LIVED

"Immediately Jesus made his disciples get into the boat and go on ahead of him to Bethsaida, while he dismissed the crowd. After leaving them, he went up on a mountainside to pray."

MARK 6:45-46

ONE MINUTE FOR YOUR FAMILY

"...as for me and my house, we will serve the Lord."

JOSHUA 24:15

To the female sex: have you ever wondered what a man most needs from the woman he loves? Some of you may think that it's love; others may say it's companionship. Many of you may say it's got to be sex. But the fact is, the answer is found in God's Word.

Ephesians Chapter 5, verse 33 says, "Let each individual among you also love his own wife as himself, and let the wife see to it that she respects her husband."

You see, God has made man and woman with just a little bit of difference in their needs. The woman most needs love, but the man's greatest need from the woman he loves is respect.

Ladies, I encourage you to remember this. You may find that your man is not only a whole lot happier, but that you receive a whole lot more love in return.

♥　　♥　　♥

WHAT A HUSBAND NEEDS MOST

"Let each individual among you also love his own wife as himself, and let the wife see to it that she respects her husband."

EPHESIANS 5: 33

> *"...Husbands ought to love their wives as their own bodies. He who loves his wife loves himself."*
>
> EPHESIANS 5: 28

WHAT A WIFE NEEDS MOST

Dr. James Dobson was asked, "Why are men so insensitive to women's needs today?" He replied, "I question whether men have really changed all that much. I doubt if men ever responded as women preferred. Did the farmer of a century ago come in from the fields to say, 'Tell me how it went with the kids today?' No. He was as oblivious to his wife's nature then as husbands are today."

So men, if you're struggling to meet your wife's needs, the Bible gives a few hints:

1. THE NEED FOR PHYSICAL AFFECTION — Not just sex but a tender touch — a few hugs throughout the day.

2. SECURITY — A wife desires a sense of security physically, financially and emotionally.

3. UNDERSTANDING — This means listening more than telling them what to do.

4. THINKING THAT SHE'S BEAUTIFUL — She needs reassurance in a society of constant comparison.

5. SPIRITUAL LEADERSHIP — Not dictatorship, but servant leadership, like Christ for His church.

Hey, let's talk maximum sex.

In a day and age of so much sexual misunderstanding, we need to look to the One who invented it. In this area, Hollywood constantly perpetuates myths and misunderstanding.

PSYCHOLOGY TODAY reported in a survey that 94% of the Soaps are about love between partners who are not married to each other. This is just the opposite of what the Inventor of sex had in mind. When God created mankind, He said, "... a man shall leave his father and mother and be united to his wife, and they will become one flesh."

1. Sex is a gift of God to be enjoyed in the context of committed love in marriage.

MAXIMUM SEX

2. Maximum sex is a by-product of a meaningful relationship with one's spouse. You are best friends, physically attracted to one another, and committed for life.

3. God's Word goes on to warn that sex outside the context of marriage is filled with problems.

So, for maximum sex, trust the Inventor of sex! He knows what's best!

♥   ♥   ♥

> "For this reason a man will leave his father and mother and be united to his wife, and they will become one flesh."
> GENESIS 2:24

> *"Train a child in the way he should go, and when he is old he will not turn from it."*
>
> PROVERBS 22:6

THE MOST DIFFICULT JOB

Have you ever considered what would be the most difficult job in life? It's the job of parenting: the challenge of guiding a child through the demands of growing up in this world and helping that child become all he or she was created to be.

The Bible provides timeless insight. "Train up a child in the way he should go, and when he is old he will not turn from it." The way he should go means according to his bent. This means we have to be students of our children — learning to recognize their God-given abilities and interests. We're also to help our children develop their strengths, as well as curb and check their weaknesses. Once we become students of our children and teach them right and wrong, with a lot of prayer thrown in, the promise of God can be realized. The challenge is a great one, but the rewards of seeing our children become mature, productive adults makes all the hard work worthwhile.

*L*et's take a moment to remember the Bible's three greatest priorities for Dads:

1. "Husbands, love your wives." The best way to be a good father is to be a loving husband. Our children need that more than anything. Remember, the Biblical word for love means more than a feeling, it means a commitment.

Ephesians 5:25

2. "Fathers, do not provoke your children to anger." Every child's psyche is fragile. We dads can expect too much at times and come down too hard on them. Worst of all, we can shut our kids out emotionally. We are to build them up and not destroy the spirit and self-image of our children.

Ephesians 6:4

3. Bring them up in the discipline and instruction of the Lord. To do this, we need to be godly men who know the Book, who live it, and teach it to our kids. Kids need to know their boundaries. It gives them security. They

DAD'S GREATEST PRIORITIES

also need instruction and teaching on what is right and wrong.

Ephesians 6:4

To sum it up, the best fathers love their wives, their kids and the Lord. Fathers, may this be our goal every single day.

♥   ♥   ♥

MOTHERHOOD

r. Leila Denmark, a well known Atlanta pediatrician, said, "Every animal on earth takes care of its own until they're able to take care of themselves, except us. We've brainwashed people into thinking that there's something greater out there than being a mother."

Ellen Wilson Fielding, who left her prestigious job as book editor of the *WALL STREET JOURNAL* to be at home full time with her son, came to see it this way: "I felt I was going to a greater thing when I left the *WALL STREET JOURNAL* to care for my son." She said, "For the essence of motherhood is the acceptance of God's offer to share in the creation and development of another human being. The question was not whether the job was good enough for me, but whether I was good enough for the job."

Motherhood is the toughest, most demanding, yet most important job in the world. With the many choices for women today, let's not forget that there's no calling of God more important than being a mom.

arents pushed and shoved their children, hoping the famous Man would touch them. His assistants, thinking they were protecting Him from unwanted demands, tried to shoo the kids away, but this important Man was indignant with his assistants. He said, "Let the children come to me." He took them in His arms, hugged them, and the kids loved Him. The man's name was Jesus. He showed His well-intentioned disciples how important children are to God.

Question: Dad... Mom... do you make time for your kids like Jesus did — the Man who lived an incredibly busy life but was not too busy for children? Very often a child's importance is shown by giving them a listening ear or a hug. A little time is all they want and need. Ask the Lord to help you be like Jesus when it comes to your kids. No job is more important than that, even if you are the Son of God.

♥   ♥   ♥

CHILDLIKE FAITH

"Let the children come to me, and do not hinder them, for the kingdom of heaven belongs to such as these."

JESUS CHRIST
MATTHEW 19:14

> *"Do not let this Book of the Law depart from your mouth; meditate on it day and night, so that you may be successful."*
>
> JOSHUA 1: 8

LEGACY

As you think of the future, I have a question. What do you plan to leave to your heirs? Stocks and bonds? Property? Investment quality art? As important as planning is for the future, there is one fact that so many fail to recognize. You're creating a legacy which will live beyond your death. Your character will continue to speak for good or evil after your life on earth has ended.

"Unquestionable character" is one of the greatest gifts we can leave our heirs. So many, by concentrating on amassing financial wealth, fail to help build honesty, responsibility, compassion or love for God and their fellowman into the life of their kids.

Character begins with your example – your life. It's more caught than taught, but teaching is important too. You can't leave your heirs a greater gift than this.

Wouldn't you like to know that your life will be remembered for more than money? What a legacy we leave our kids when they reflect on our life and say, "You know my Mom or my Dad, why, that's the finest person I've ever known."

Mark Twain said, "When a child turns thirteen, put them in a barrel and feed them through a hole. When they get to be sixteen, plug up the hole." That's not a very positive view of parenting teens but one that everyone can relate to, for parenting teens isn't easy.

David Gelman writes, "Today's teenagers face more adult-strength stresses than their predecessors did — at a time when adults are much less available to help them." So here are a few suggestions:

1. *Education is not the goal; wisdom is.* Education helps, but teaching kids to sort out information is the key.

2. *Teach them how to take care of their bodies with a good diet and good exercise.* Remember safe sex isn't safe, only abstinence is.

3. *Help them develop a relationship with God.* Recognize that much of their development will come from the relationship with God they see in you.

4. *Teach them that there are moral absolutes based on scrip-*

> "*And Jesus grew in wisdom and stature, and in favor with God and men.*"
> LUKE 2:52

PARENTING TEENS ISN'T EASY

ture. Teens need these guidelines.

5. *Help them make wise decisions about the company they keep.* Positive peer pressure is a key.

6. *Pray* — Teens and parents of teens need lots of prayer!

> "*I have no greater joy than this, to hear of my children walking in the truth.*"
>
> III JOHN 1: 4

LETTING GO AS A PARENT

There has been an emotional moment that my wife and I have experienced with all of our boys. It happened when we walked each of them to the bus stop to begin first grade. We knew the first stage of parenting (the pre-school years) was over.

Now it's happened again as our oldest son has left home for college. Really, the whole parenting process is one of letting go. Let me make a few suggestions:

1. Do whatever you can to allow mom to be at home full-time with the children in the preschool years. I realize single parents don't have this option, but if you can work it out — do it. This short-term sacrifice brings long-term results.

2. Love them always and let them know of your love for them.

3. Discipline them consistently so that they will know there are consequences for stepping over the line.

4. Pray for them regularly that they'll make wise choices and that their influences are for good.

Letting go is not easy, but with God's help and our love, our children can grow to be responsible adults.

There are not many qualities more important than honoring our parents. It's a biggie; one of God's Big Ten Commandments.

The Bible says: "Honor your father and mother, so that you may live long in the land the Lord your God is giving you." It's obvious that the future of our land depends on our faithfulness to this command.

So what's the practical application? How is it carried out throughout life? Well, it comes in three stages:

1. The first stage calls for obedience. Children are called to obey their parents as long as they live in the home with them and/or financially depend on them.

HONORING OUR PARENTS

2. The second stage begins in the young adult years. It lasts much of our adult life, when we're out on our own. During these years, the way we honor our parents is through respect.

3. The third stage comes when our parents are older and unable to care for themselves. Then, the way we honor them is to care for them and to see that their needs are met. This is perhaps the most neglected stage in American life.

> "Honor your father and your mother, so that you may live long in the land the Lord your God is giving you."
> EXODUS 20:12

Obedience, then respect, and finally, care, are three stages of honoring our parents. Let's take this seriously because the very future of our land depends on it.

♥   ♥   ♥

> *"If you obey my commands, you will remain in My love; just as I have obeyed My Father's commands, and remain in His love."*
>
> JESUS CHRIST
> JOHN 15:10

OBEDIENCE

Parents, what is the greatest proof of your child's love for you? Is it when they say they love you? That's great, but it's not proof. Really, it's when they obey you — willingly.

Many people miss this truth. They say they love God, maybe even go to church regularly, but there's little evidence of real love for God in their lives.

A recent poll showed that 80% of Americans believe that the Bible is the inspired Word of God. That same poll reflected the view that more than 70% felt every individual has to decide right or wrong for himself. That's saying one thing and doing another.

Jesus said, "If you love Me, you will keep My commandments." The proof of our love for God is our willingness to obey God and His commands. Doesn't it make you feel great when your child willingly obeys you? Why don't you give God the same joy. Obey Him because it's your desire to do so. Love Him like you want to be loved by your own child.

Perhaps the toughest stage of parenting is parenting our parents. It's a role reversal in the adult child's life that both the parent and the child would rather not face. The Bible clearly teaches us to honor our parents, and that means caring for them when they are old. Let me suggest a few thoughts:

1. The greatest gift you can give your aging parents is time, but if physical distance is great, take time to call or write on a regular basis.

2. Be prayerful and sensitive when parents can no longer care for themselves or their home. Be honest in helping them think about where they'll live — be it a retirement center, a nursing home, or with you.

PARENTING OUR PARENTS

3. As you face these tough decisions, be motivated by love not guilt. Do what they most need, not what you most want.

Honoring our parents sometimes means parenting our parents. Remember, we reap what we sow. One day we hope that our children will have learned FROM us how best to care FOR us when we are old.

♥   ♥   ♥

> "Even to your old age, I shall be the same. And even to your graying years I shall bear you."
>
> ISAIAH 46: 4

> *"Marriage should be honored by all."*
> HEBREWS
> 13:4A

DIVORCE PREVENTION

Everybody likes to be thought of as NUMBER ONE. Every football season, many fans will chant their team is NUMBER ONE! America is a nation that prides itself on being NUMBER ONE in many categories, but we are number one in a category that is not good: NUMBER ONE in divorce. One out of every two marriages ends in divorce.

When Jesus was asked about divorce, He made it clear that it was never what God had in mind. Then, He quickly began to talk about marriage and the commitment that is involved. Obviously, a marriage that lasts a lifetime is what God desires. So let me suggest 12 words for you and your spouse to live by: words which help with DIVORCE PREVENTION.

"I love you."

"I admire you."

"I was wrong."

"Please forgive me."

Expressing love and admiration, admitting when we are wrong, and asking forgiveness are the ingredients for divorce prevention. Wouldn't it be great if, one day, America became number one in marriages that last!

Very often people who face divorce feel hopeless, and, sadly, many who turn to the church for help feel rejected, not welcomed. Many have told me they felt outcast and shunned, even if they were the spouse left behind. Sometimes this is a perception, but sometimes it is very real. Sadly, the Christian army is the only army in the world known to shoot its wounded.

Yes, Scripture teaches that God hates divorce, but just because He hates divorce doesn't mean He hates the divorcee. He loves the divorcee. God hates divorce for many of the same reasons the divorcee hates divorce — most of all, for the pain and suffering that results in so many lives. There is no doubt that divorce always results from sin, but it is not the unforgivable sin.

Divorce is never what God wants, but Jesus teaches us that we have a God of second chances — a God of forgiveness. When we trust in Christ, and confess our sins to the Lord, we begin to realize He loves us and forgives us completely. We can find that total and complete healing in the person of Jesus Christ.

HOPE AFTER DIVORCE

> *"If we confess our sins, He is faithful and righteous to forgive us our sins and to cleanse us from all unrighteousness."*
>
> I JOHN 1:9

♥ ♥ ♥

ONE MINUTE FOR

O THERS

"...with humility
of mind let each
of you regard
one another as
more important
than himself;
do not merely
look out for your
own personal
interests, but also
for the interests
of others."

PHILIPPIANS 2:3-4

Who really knows you... the thoughts of your heart and the secret things that you intentionally keep hidden from others? Do you share your innermost thoughts with anyone? Some may say it's their spouse or a best friend. Yet, I suggest that even though you may think that you know yourself well and that others see the real you, no one knows you more completely than the One who created you.

God says, "Before I formed you in the womb I knew you." It only makes sense that, in order to know and understand ourselves, we need a personal relationship with the One who knows us best.

The good news is that God knows us best, and He loves us more than anyone else. He knows our failings and our shortcomings and He loves us anyway. Through Jesus Christ, we have the privilege of having a personal relationship with our Creator. That relationship begins when we accept God's love through faith. It's a relationship that lasts forever and that's mighty good news.

♥   ♥   ♥

WHO KNOWS YOU?

"Before I formed you in the womb I knew you. Before you were born I set you apart; I appointed you as a prophet to the nations."

JEREMIAH 1:5

> "*A friend loves at all times....*"
>
> PROVERBS
> 17:17

FRIENDS

What is your definition of true friendship? Ralph Waldo Emerson once said: "Happy is the house that shelters a friend," and "a friend is a person with whom I may be sincere, and before him I may think aloud. The only reward of virtue is virtue and the only way to have a friend is to be one."

Walter Winchell defines a friend as "one who walks in when others walk out." Someone else has said that a friend is "a man who laughs at your funny stories, even when they ain't so good, and sympathizes with your misfortunes, even when they ain't so bad."

Do you have a friend? Do you know true friendship? Many, I'm sad to say, would have to answer no. The good news is this: You can have a Best Friend forever and that Friend is Jesus Christ. I encourage you to get to know Him; you'll never be disappointed. He'll always be there with you.

 ♥ ♥ ♥

A real friend is one of life's greatest blessings. In this day of temporary relationships, true friendship is rare. The challenge is how can you find and develop lasting friendships? The Bible gives us some guidance:

♥ To have a friend, you must be a friend. Go out of your way to show that you are interested in their lives. Ask questions and take time to listen to their answers.

♥ To cement a friendship, be loyal. Demonstrate your willingness to love them unconditionally, even when your friend is not lovable. Be supportive, even when your friend is not popular.

♥ To experience lasting friendship, be an encourager. A true friend is someone who will tell you the truth, but always with your best interest at heart.

It's been said, to have as many true friends as the fingers on your hands is a great blessing. To have just one or two is great as well.

♥   ♥   ♥

FRIENDSHIP

"...There is a friend who sticks closer than a brother."

PROVERBS
18:24

> "But the Lord said to Samuel, 'Do not consider his appearance or his height, for I have rejected him. The Lord does not look at the things man looks at. Man looks at the outward appearance, but the Lord looks at the heart.'"
>
> I SAMUEL 16:7

HOW GOD MEASURES A MAN

How do you measure the worth of another person? Is it by their wealth, their position, their fame, their looks, their education, or their success?

I don't know how you'd answer that question, but I can tell you how God measures the worth of a person. God's Word says, "God does not see man as man sees him. For man looks at the outward appearance, but the Lord looks at the heart."

The heart speaks of a person's character, their courage and their spirit. So often when we measure the worth of a person we just look at the outward appearance, but God looks at the inside.

If that's the case, how does He measure you? If you had a heart exam today, what kind of heart would God find? The good news is this: God has given us a way to have a new heart and it's found through faith in Jesus Christ.

It's an interesting insight of life that, when we begin to have the right heart through Christ, we begin to measure the worth of others God's way.

♥　　♥　　♥

Imagine that you need surgery to remove a splinter of wood from your eye. One slip of the scalpel and you are ruined. The doctor tells you that the surgery will be no problem, but something about the doctor is so horrifying as to be comical. You notice he's got a two-by-four through both his eyes.

That ludicrous scene is what Jesus was illustrating when He talked about judging others. He said, "Do not judge or you too will be judged....Why do you look at the speck of sawdust in your brother's eye, and pay no attention to the plank in your own eye....You hypocrite! First take the plank out of your own eye, and then you will see clearly to remove the speck from your brother's eye."

In short, we are often blind to our own flaws in judging the flaws of others. It's ludicrous to get in the judging business, for none of us have good enough vision to know the whole story. Only God sees with complete vision. He's the only One with 20/20 vision in understanding another person's life. Let's get into the loving business and leave the judging up to God.

♥　　♥　　♥

JUDGING OTHERS

"Do not judge, or you too will be judged. For in the same way you judge others, you will be judged, and with the measure you use, it will be measured to you. Why do you look at the speck of sawdust in your brother's eye and pay no attention to the plank in your own eye? You hypocrite, first take the plank out of your own eye, and then you will see clearly to remove the speck from your brother's eye."

JESUS CHRIST
MATTHEW 7:1-3,5

> *"You have heard that it was said, 'Love your neighbor and hate your enemy.' But I tell you: 'Love your enemies and pray for those who persecute you.'"*
>
> JESUS CHRIST
> MATTHEW 5:43,44

DESTROYING OUR ENEMIES

The word "enemy" has been defined as anyone who is not for us. In light of that definition we can all think of folks we work with, cross paths with, and sometimes even live with, who are not for us. Yet Jesus Christ said, "Love your enemies." To love our friends is not unique, but to love our enemies is.

At the end of the Civil War, many Northerners were demanding that the South be punished for the devastation the War had caused the US. In the midst of this issue, a group visited President Lincoln in the White House, feeling he was being too soft on the South. One man became so intense that he pounded on Mr. Lincoln's desk and he said, "Mr. President, I believe in destroying my enemies."

President Lincoln reflected a moment, then slowly stood and said this, "Do we not destroy our enemies when we make them our friends?"

That is true Christianity that literally changes the world. The question is, is it you?

♥ ♥ ♥

In 1962 in Montgomery, Alabama, a young, unknown Baptist preacher came home to find a large crowd gathered in front of his house that had just been bombed.

He quickly ran inside to see if his wife and daughter had survived. Miraculously, he found that they had not been harmed. He comforted them before going back outside to the large angry crowd.

They had gathered with chains and weapons to retaliate against the white community for such a despicable deed. He told them there would be no retaliation,

"Jesus tells us to love our enemies, to forgive those who persecute us. Now go home." Thus, the legend of Martin Luther King, Jr. began — an amazing man, with a unique spirit.

My friends, what M.L. King did on that occasion isn't natural; it's supernatural. The ability to forgive our enemies who have wronged us is often beyond our natural ability, but it is the Spirit of Christ. It is true Christianity. It is a power available to us all that can change the world.

♥   ♥   ♥

FORGIVING OUR ENEMIES

"Be kind and compassionate to one another, forgiving each other, just as in Christ God forgave you."
EPHESIANS 4:32

> *"...whoever spreads slander is a fool."*
>
> PROVERBS 10:18

THE FACTS VS. THE TRUTH IN GOSSIP

A pastor went to visit a woman in his church before serious surgery. As he walked into her hospital room, he found her in the arms of a man who was not her husband. Stunned and embarrassed, he silently walked out. Later he discovered that this woman's brother had flown in from California to comfort her before her surgery.

The pastor later said, "I could have told others I saw that woman in the arms of a man who was not her husband and it would have been the facts, but it would not have been the truth."

The press often does this in reporting what people have done. They confuse the facts with the truth. This results in half-truths which really are the worst form of lies, for they are so believable. Gossip and slander are big on facts and short on truth. They destroy people's character unfairly.

So the next time you hear something bad about another person, be sure you have more than the facts. Be sure you have the whole truth, for it is easy to confuse the facts with the truth.

One of life's most common oversights is not taking time to say thanks. We get in such a rush that we often forget.

Years ago, 10 men with the dreaded disease of leprosy saw Jesus. They were a long distance away, for leprosy was the most feared diseased of that day. They were outcasts; people didn't want to touch them for fear of getting the disease. They were treated then like many today who have AIDS.

These lepers cried out to Christ to have mercy on them, and He did. He healed them all. What a fantastic day that must have been!

Those 10 guys got so excited that they all began to run and tell what had happened.

But, one of them turned around and took time to worship and thank Jesus — just one. Jesus asked him, "Weren't there ten? Where are they?" Even God desires to hear "Thanks."

This week, don't miss a great opportunity to get in the habit of taking time to say thanks... to God for His blessings... to friends and loved ones... and to any who help you along the way.

Jesus and the Ten Healed of Leprosy

THANKSGIVING

LUKE
17:11-19

> *"In everything give thanks, for this is God's will for you in Christ Jesus."*
>
> I THESSALONIANS 5:18

APPRECIATION

Have you ever given a gift or done a favor for someone who did not express appreciation? It's not much fun and certainly doesn't inspire us to give to that person again. But if we're honest, we all have to admit that we all have failed to say thank you.

Think about the people in service positions that we encounter daily. Do you thank the folks at the dry cleaners when your shirts are ready when they promised? How about saying thanks to the person behind the counter in the fast food restaurant? Do you express appreciation to the people in your office who answer the phone or process the mail?

Everyone likes to be appreciated, to hear "thank you" for things they have done well. Why not start today saying thanks to the people who make your day run so smoothly? While you're at it, thank God for all His blessings in your life.

Saying "thank you" is always appreciated. It sure makes the day a bit brighter.

♥   ♥   ♥

It is always appropriate that we take a moment to remember those who have put their lives on the line to preserve our freedom and to give thanks for those who have given their lives for their country. Jesus said, "Greater love has no one than this, that one lay down his life for his friend."

We should especially honor those who served in Viet Nam. Never has our nation acted so shamefully as it did to the men and women in uniform who served in that conflict. They served in a war they did not start to preserve freedom for those they did not know, yet time and again our soldiers returned home, only to be spat upon by citizens of this land.

Chances are, you know someone who served in Viet Nam and never considered the trauma they faced, not only in war, but being caught in the crossfire of a nation divided when they returned home. Always honor those who have given their lives for their nation, but let us especially take time to thank those who put their lives on the line in Viet Nam.

If you were one who served, I salute you. If you know someone who did, it's time to say THANKS.

> "*Greater love has no one than this, that he lay down his life for his friend.*"
> JESUS CHRIST
> JOHN 15:13

MEMORIAL DAY

CAN'T LEGISLATE MORALITY

> "But we know that the law is good, if one uses it lawfully, realizing the fact that law is not made for a righteous man, but for those who are lawless and rebellious...."
>
> I TIMOTHY 1:8-9

One of the leaders of the Georgia General Assembly, in opposition to House Ethics legislation, was quoted as saying this, "You can't legislate morality." Have you ever used that argument, "Can't legislate morality?" I ask you, why do those guys meet? To make laws! Has there ever been a law written that wasn't legislating morality?

Yes, I know what they mean; laws don't guarantee proper behavior. Any law can be broken, but they sure do make people think twice before breaking them.

Laws of the state are part of God's plan for man protecting himself from one another. So, next time someone says you can't legislate morality, just suggest they do away with laws on rape... murder... robbery. Sure, laws don't change a person's heart — only Jesus Christ can do that — but they sure do help us protect ourselves from our fellow man.

When Israel and the PLO signed the peace treaty on the White House lawn, it was an amazing moment. Time will tell if a peace treaty works, for peace in our world is illusive and difficult to grasp.

Remember, peace is not the absence of conflict; that's a truce. Peace is a reconciliation between two estranged parties. Reconciliation means to become one, or to become friends, which is very different from a truce.

In that light, I propose to you that man will never find lasting peace until he finds peace within himself, and, we can't find peace within until we find peace with God. That peace is found through the person of Jesus Christ.

Christ did not come to bring peace on earth through peace treaties, but He came to reconcile sinful individuals with God. With that comes inner peace, and with inner peace comes the ability to live at peace with our fellow man.

♥   ♥   ♥

> "Peace I leave with you; My peace I give you. I do not give to you as the world gives…"
>
> PEACE
>
> JESUS CHRIST
> JOHN 14:27

SELF-MADE MAN

DAVID
PSALM 147

There's no such thing as a self-made man. It's an American myth. The fact is, we are all indebted to someone.

Think about it. Most of you were born in America. Did you have any part in that decision? Did you write the Constitution that guarantees you freedom to live and work where you choose? Did you have anything to do with our nation's abundant natural resources?

What about the people that helped you along the way — a relative, a teacher, a coach, a friend or a mentor? The fact is, there is no one that can really call themselves a self-made man or woman. We are all indebted to someone.

I urge you to take a few moments to say thanks to someone who has encouraged you along the way through a phone call, a note, or a visit. As you do, don't forget your Maker who has allowed you to be a part of this land we call America; the land of the free and the land of opportunity. How much God has blessed us through our land and for that we can be forever grateful.

I'm just curious...

Why is it in a culture increasingly obsessed with the environment and protecting all species that so many of these same folks are for destroying the lives of unborn children?

I'm just curious....

Why is it that value-free sex education, that teaches safe sex to save lives, is advising young people on an unsafe approach that could kill them? Entrusting your life to a thin rubber shield, when the failure rate is so high, is bewildering indeed.

I'm just curious....

Why is it that when a Buddhist monk prays like a Buddhist, he sounds wise and noble, but a Christian who prays in Jesus' name is insensitive and offensive?

I'm just curious....

Why is it in a culture where the supreme virtue is often tolerance, so many are so intolerant of the name of Jesus Christ or Biblical convictions? Just curious.

Don't things like this make you just a little bit curious too?

♥   ♥   ♥

I'M JUST CURIOUS

"They are darkened in their understanding, and separated from the life of God, because of the ignorance that is in them due to the hardening of their hearts."

EPHESIANS 4:18

ONE MINUTE FOR

*G*OD

"...serve God
with a whole heart
and a willing
mind; for the
Lord searches all
hearts and
understands every
intent of the
thoughts. If you
seek Him,
He will let you
find Him."

I CHRONICLES 28:9

I love the fall... the excitement of football season, the crisp coolness of the morning air, the beauty of the changing leaves. This time of year really invigorates me. It's easy to be enthusiastic about life when the world around us is so colorful.

The changing of the seasons reminds us that God created a universe where there is order; fall follows summer every year. The seasons come like clockwork. So dependable is the change, that we take it for granted. The Bible tells us that, even if we had no other way of knowing that there is a God, nature alone is enough proof of His existence. Creation

THE CREATOR REVEALED

shows us God's power and so much of His divine nature.

As you enjoy the change of seasons each year, I hope you will acknowledge the Creator of such beauty and majesty. He is a God of order in creation, and yet best of all, His greatest desire is to have a personal relationship with you.

♥   ♥   ♥

> *"For since the creation of the world God's invisible qualities - his eternal power and divine nature - have been clearly seen, being understood from what has been made, so that men are without excuse."*
> ROMANS 1:20

> *"Lift up your eyes on high, and see who has created these stars, the One who leads forth their host by number... the Everlasting God, the Lord, the Creator of the ends of the earth."*
>
> ISAIAH 40:26, 28

IS THERE OTHER LIFE IN THE UNIVERSE?

America's spaceship on Mars produced magnificent views of space. Scientists are seeing unlimited potential for space exploration and their excitement is contagious. There's so much more to know and explore!

Could there be life on other planets? How do these new discoveries affect our view of God? Do we need to revise our understanding of Him? Well, the answer depends on how big your concept of God is. You see, we need to recognize that God is almighty, far greater than anything the human mind can conceive. The discoveries of science excite us, but it is even more exciting when we recognize the greatness of the Creator of it all. God is limitless. His creative genius surpasses man's ability to comprehend.

We don't need to fear science or what's out there in space, for, in the end, science simply explains to us the Creative genius of God. God is over all!

One day Dr. Charles Allen, the famous Methodist minister, was asked by one of his members, "Who was the greatest president America ever had?" He quickly responded, "Lyndon Johnson."

The member was furious. "Dr. Allen how can you say such a thing about a lying, scheming scoundrel?" Allen said, "The answer's simple. One day I was standing in a Houston hotel and President Johnson walked through. He asked, 'Dr. Allen, are you keeping all the Methodists straight?' I said, 'I'm doing my best, Mr. President.' You see, he's the only president to call me by

HE KNOWS YOUR NAME

my name. I like a president who knows my name."

Think about it. When we're at the airport and someone is paged, we hardly notice. But, when our name is called, it immediately gets our attention.

Having a president who knows your name would make anyone feel important, but you can do even better than that. God's word

> "...*I know my own,
> and my own know me.*"
>
> JESUS
> CHRIST
> JOHN
> 10:14

tells us that the Creator of the universe knows your name. The King of Kings even knows the number of hairs on your head. So, the key question is, "Why don't you get to know Him?" Believe it or not, that's what He desires most of all.

> "As the Father has love me, so have I loved you. Now remain in my love."
>
> JESUS CHRIST
> JOHN 15:9

CASUAL LOVE

Love... how often we use the word. We love warm weather, our husband or wife, our college football team, the latest fashion trend. We speak the word in our tenderest moments and then use it to describe our feelings about a flavor of ice cream

Do you know that you are loved - really loved? The God who created all of life loves you, even if you don't love Him in return. He doesn't wait for you to demonstrate your love for Him, He loves you first of all — even before you know He's around.

Over the next few days, try to notice how many times the word "love" is used in casual conversation. Each time you hear it, think about the love of God, how much He loves you, and begin to experience His love. When you begin to love Him in return, you'll be amazed at the joy in your own life.

♥   ♥   ♥

One day a bird, caught in our chimney, flew into our house. We tried desperately to get it out the door, but it didn't seem to get the message. After a while, totally frustrated, I had the ridiculous thought, "If I could become a bird for a few seconds and talk its language, I could show it how to be free." Then I remembered that God did just that.

The Creator of the universe became one of His own creatures, a man, in order to communicate perfectly with mankind. Jesus took on a human body and personality with all its limitations so that you and I could understand how to be free to live and have a relationship with God.

This is really what Christmas is all about. God chose to reveal Himself to us in the form of a baby, Jesus Christ. When you get to know the God who loves us so much that He would humble Himself to become a man, then Christmas always has a sense of wonder.

THE CREATOR AND HIS CREATURES

> *"For God So loved the world that He gave his one and only Son that whoever believes in Him shall not perish but have eternal life."*
>
> JOHN 3:16

> *"...the water I shall give him shall become in him a well of water springing up to eternal life."*
>
> JESUS CHRIST
> JOHN 4:14

WATER IN THE DESERT

If you've ever traveled through the desert, you'll notice that it's mile after mile of dry and barren landscape. Then suddenly, there's a spot of green, some trees, bushes and flowering plants. It always means there is some kind of water source nearby. With water, the desert blossoms and comes to life.

The same is true in our lives. Without God, we tend to dry up when life gets hard. It saps us of all our energy, creativity and drive.

We eventually feel beaten down, worn out and dried up, but Jesus says, "I am living water; anyone who accepts me will never be thirsty again." He wasn't talking about physical thirst. He was talking about satisfying our spiritual thirst so we can blossom and come to life.

What about it? Do you sometimes feel like a dry, dusty shrub in a desert of emptiness? Come to Christ and enjoy a cool drink of water whenever you need it.

Have you ever noticed how noise fills our lives? We wake to music or alarms. We get in the car and what's the first thing we do? Flip in a tape or CD or turn on the radio. When we walk in the house or a hotel room, the first thing we do is turn on the TV. It just seems that with noise, we don't feel so alone.

In the midst of all of this noise, are you missing the most important voice of all? God still speaks in a still, small voice. In the busyness and loudness of our lives, it's easy to miss Him. The only way to hear Him is to make an intentional effort to quiet the noise of our life and spend some time listening through prayer and reading His Word. You will never get a more important phone call or crucial message.

Find some time each day to be alone and quiet, and listen to the most important voice of all. It will enrich your life tremendously.

♥   ♥   ♥

NOISE

"Give ear and hear my voice, listen and hear my words."

ISAIAH 28:23

> "If we confess our sins,
> He is faithful and
> righteous
> to forgive
> us our sins, and to
> cleanse us from all
> unrighteousness."
>
> I JOHN 1:9

TRUTH OR CONSEQUENCES

There was a game show in the early days of television called *Truth or Consequences.* Contestants had to answer questions correctly or face embarrassing consequences.

The Bible is a book of truth and consequences; it tells the truth about God and how to live. It also makes the consequences of ignoring God's teaching very clear. In it we read the stories of people who failed to obey God's guidelines and the tragic results of their failure to do so.

We also read that God provided a way for all of us to escape the inevitable consequences of sin. Jesus Christ, through His perfect life and sacrificial death, paid the price for our sin. He will not remove the consequences of wrongdoing here on earth, but He does forgive us and remove the eternal consequences of our sin.

The big question for your life is "Will you believe the truth, or face the consequences?" The decision is yours.

A common question is "How can a loving God allow so much suffering and evil in the world?" It's a tough question that philosophers and theologians have struggled with forever. There is no completely adequate answer, but it is important to remember that God is blamed for a lot of things that man does wrong.

When God created man He gave us all a free will. He didn't program us as robots to always do what is right or what He wants. Robots have no choice, but humans do. We can choose to trust and obey God — or do things our own way.

From the first man and woman, each person has chosen to go his or her own way rather than God's way. The result of man's sin is disease, suffering and death.

God has done something pretty dramatic to confront the problem. He humbled Himself to become one of us in the person of Jesus Christ to show us how to live. Even more, Christ came to

WHY DOES GOD ALLOW SUFFERING?

> "For as through the one man's disobedience the many were made sinners, even so through the obedience of the one the many will be made righteous."
>
> ROMANS 5:19

die for us. Through faith in Him, we begin to reverse this cycle of evil and suffering.

♥　　♥　　♥

> *"No one is justified by the law before God; for, the righteous man shall live by faith."*
>
> GALATIANS 2:16

WHY RELIGION STINKS

A common complaint in life is to hear that more problems have been brought on in this world from religion than anything else. I used to feel defensive, even embarrassed, when people would make that charge. Now, I don't, because I've come to realize that Christianity is not a religion — it's a relationship with God through Jesus Christ.

Religion is about works... rituals and rules to EARN favor with God. Christianity is just the opposite, for there is no way we can ever be good enough to earn God's favor. We all blow it. We all fall short. If you are going to try and make it to Heaven on good works, the Bible says you have to be perfect — always!

I know that's impossible for me. That's why I'm thankful that Christianity is about faith; faith that Jesus' death on the cross is the key to receiving God's grace and eternal life. We can't earn it; it's a gift. So why don't you accept it on faith and begin a relationship with God today.

What is your purpose for living? Have you ever taken time to pause in the rat race of life and figure out why you're in it? I recommend developing a life purpose statement. A man once told me his purpose statement was "Get all you can; can all you get; and sit on the can!" I hope when you develop your purpose statement it'll be more than that.

Don't be so short-sighted, focusing on this life alone. Keep eternity in mind, for all of us have really been created by God for a purpose. What's yours? Here's a hint: to know why God has put you on this earth becomes clear when you get to know the person of Jesus Christ.

PURPOSE FOR LIVING

With Him, it's amazing how all things become clear; otherwise, you wind up like the masses — too busy to take time to know why you're here — too lost to know where you're going.

Are you racing through life — going nowhere fast? Stop for a second. Look to God in Christ and discover the purpose of your life.

♥   ♥   ♥

> "He who has the Son has the life; he who does not have the Son of God does not have the Life."
> I JOHN 5:12

SUPERNATURAL BIRTH

*I*magine this... your high school honey that you love and believe is a good person because she doesn't believe in sex before marriage, comes up to you and says, "I'm pregnant but don't be mad 'cause I'm still a virgin." Now, how would you respond?

Here's the kicker — this scenario really happened a long time ago, about 2000 years ago. In fact, the guy was named Joe and his pregnant girlfriend was named Mary. She went on to tell him that God had caused her to become pregnant.

At first, Joe didn't believe Mary and he decided to drop her. Then an angel appeared to Joe and let him know Mary was telling the truth. So he stayed with her, believing the Lord in faith.

Really, for the rational, secular, scientific mind of the 1990s, this story is incredible. But, it's the story of Christmas — the story of Jesus' birth. The question is: Do you believe it? Be it Jesus' birth or His resurrection, I want you to know you've got to believe it fully to experience the wonder of Christmas.

♥   ♥   ♥

Do you know the most common objection to Christianity? Number 1? Top of the charts every year? It goes like this (maybe you've said it yourself): "I'm not interested in Christianity or the church because the church is a bunch of hypocrites and I don't want to have anything to do with them."

Do you know what? If you've said that, you're exactly right. The church is full of hypocrites, but I can't think of a better place for a bunch of hypocrites to be than in church. You see, the church is not a hotel for saints; it's a hospital for sinners. It's a place where people go when they recognize they need some help.

HYPOCRITES

Let me encourage you to do this: instead of blaming Jesus Christ for the shortcomings of His followers, look at the person of Jesus Christ in Scripture. You'll find no phoniness, or lack of sincerity in Him. Look at the person of Christ and you'll find the most genuine person who has ever lived.

♥　　♥　　♥

"...Christ also suffered for you, leaving you an example for you to follow in His steps, who committed no sin, nor was any deceit found in His mouth; and while being reviled, He did not revile in return...."

I PETER 2: 21-23

> *Nicodemus said to Jesus: "How can a man be born when he is old? He cannot enter a second time into his mother's womb and be born, can he?"*
>
> FIND OUT HOW
> JESUS ANSWERED HIM IN
> THE BOOK OF
> JOHN, CHAPTER 3

BORN AGAIN

Do you hear the term BORN AGAIN and immediately think of a type of person you don't want to be? A type of Christian that often seems narrow and self-righteous? Somebody just too "religious" for your taste? Sadly, sometimes these negative qualities are all too real. Do you have any idea where the term originated? It comes right out of Scripture, from Jesus Christ Himself.

Jesus tells a man named Nic that unless he is born again, he'll never enter God's Kingdom.

What did He mean? Basically this. Just as all people have a physical birth, all people need to have a spiritual birth to become a child of God and to be in God's Kingdom forever.

How does one become born again? Why don't you find out for yourself? You can read the story in John 3 in the Bible. See what Jesus says first hand. Come on, don't be chicken! I dare you! Open that closed mind of yours and read it for yourself. John, Chapter 3. Have you got guts enough to read it and decide if it's true?

Why do Christians believe they have the only way to God? Aren't all religions basically the same? Actually, they are not. Can you show me the founder of any other faith who claimed to be God and backed up his claim by rising from the dead? Oh, many gurus and cult leaders have claimed to be God and, when they die, their followers believe they'll come back to life, but none ever have.

You see, it is Jesus Himself who said, "I am the Way... the Truth... the Life... no one comes to the Father but through Me." Christians believe what Jesus says is true because of His resurrection.

If the exclusive aspect of Christianity bothers you, why don't you seek to disprove Jesus' resurrection? If it didn't happen, Jesus is one of the biggest liars or lunatics to ever walk the earth. Furthermore, His followers are to be pitied as a deceived bunch. Whatever you do, don't claim Jesus is just another good, religious leader. Either He tells the truth or He doesn't. Good people don't lie and deceive. Good people tell the truth.

♥   ♥   ♥

ONLY ONE WAY TO GOD?

"But small is the gate and narrow the road that leads to life, and only a few find it."

JESUS CHRIST
MATTHEW 7:1 4

> *"The Father Himself loves you, because you have loved Me and have believed that I came from God."*
>
> JESUS CHRIST
> JOHN 16:27

VISIT TO THE WHITE HOUSE

If you were to drive up to the gates of the White House today and tell them that you wanted to see the president, do you think they'd let you in? Fat chance for most of us. But, let me tell you what happened to a friend of mine who was invited to the White House by President Ford's son when Ford was in office. He said it was amazing.

They came to the White House gates and the guards waved them through. They entered the White House with no one stopping them. They even walked right into the Oval Office unhindered. Then President Ford stood up, welcomed his son, then looked my friend in the eye and said, "Any friend of my son is welcome here."

That's exactly how it will be getting into heaven. The only way we'll have access is by knowing God's son; otherwise, it will be more futile than trying to get into the White House without the right credentials.

Do you know God's son personally? He really is the key for entrance into heaven.

Almost two thousand years ago, a man named Pilate asked the most important question in life. Standing before him was an itinerant preacher. There was nothing remarkable about His looks. He had attracted a large following, but few committed followers. He had no wealth, not even a home of His own, yet He was the object of unmitigated hatred from a mob.

Pilate asked, "What shall I do with this man?" As the mob cried for His execution, the man stood silently as Pilate, the cowardly politician, sentenced Him to death on a cross.

The question Pilate asked is ultimately one all of us have to ask as well. What shall I do with the man, this man Jesus? I promise you - He loves you even when you could care less about Him. He cared enough to give His life for you. What will you do with Jesus?

Pilate tried to get rid of Him, but it couldn't be done. What will you with this Man? Your eternal destiny hangs in the balance by how you respond.

❤   ❤   ❤

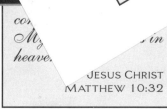

LIFE'S M
IMPORTANT QU

co...
My...
heave...

...in

"Becau...
seen...

JESUS CHRIST
MATTHEW 10:32

EVIDENCE FOR THE RESURRECTION

What is some of the evidence for the resurrection of Jesus Christ? The church's existence to this day. Do you realize that only one fact gave the early church its power? The resurrection of Jesus. When Jesus died on the cross, His followers left Him, fleeing for their lives, yet something occurred to empower them with great faith. The church has survived, in spite of almost 2000 years of so much sorry preaching.

People continue to experience the risen Christ living in them.

Sunday is the day of worship. How can you explain a group of Jewish people who revere the Sabbath, changing the day of worship from Saturday to Sunday? Sunday became known as the Lord's Day for Jesus rose from the dead that day.

If the resurrection doesn't account for this, what does? None of this proves the resurrection, but it is evidence that must be explored.

In looking at the resurrection of Jesus Christ, there are many theories espoused to debunk it. Let me share with you one of the funniest that tries to explain the empty tomb. It's called the Swoon Theory.

This theory argues that Jesus really didn't die. The Roman guards thought he had died, but He was just unconscious (or swooned) from the loss of blood and exhaustion on the cross. Later, He revived and came out of the tomb and appeared to His disciples who thought He had risen.

Yeah, sure. After the ordeal of the crucifixion in losing all of His blood, He survived three days without food or water in a damp tomb, unwrapped His tightly bound grave clothes, rolled away the heavy stone and overcame the Roman guards. Then He walked miles on feet that had been spiked.

It takes more faith to believe this theory than to believe the resurrection. In the end, the only theory that explains the empty tomb is Jesus' resurrection from the dead.

♥   ♥   ♥

THE FUNNIEST THEORY

"...The Son of Man must suffer many things and be rejected by the elders, the chief priests and scribes, and be killed, and after three days rise again."

JESUS CHRIST
MARK 8: 31

> "And, if Christ has not been raised, then our preaching is vain, your faith is also in vain."
>
> I CORINTHIANS 15: 14

THE EMPTY TOMB

If you're a skeptic about the resurrection of Jesus, how do you explain the "empty tomb?"

Some say the disciples stole the body. Matthew 28:11-15 speaks of this rumor.

I ask you (a) how could they overcome the Roman guards who were executed if they left their post or lost their prisoner. and (b) how can you explain all the disciples dying a martyr's death, at different locations and times, for proclaiming something that they knew to be a lie?

People will die for a lie if they don't know its a lie, but people don't die for something they know is untrue. Do you remember Watergate... all those Nixon loyalists running for their lawyers when they realized prison might be ahead?

All the disciples had to do to escape martyrdom was renounce their claim that Jesus Christ proved He is God's son by rising from the dead. They did not. No, the disciples didn't steal Jesus' body. They died because they knew that Jesus rose.

What is Heaven like? The most common image is a place of clouds where people wear white robes, halos and do nothing except play a harp with a goofy smile on their faces. That's a view of Heaven that sounds more like Hell to me! What a bore!

What is Heaven really like? Jesus spoke very little of it, but He did say this, "In My Father's house are many dwelling places. I go to prepare a place for you." What is heaven like? It's like home — with a loving Father. Heaven is like home — like home ought to be: a place of security; a permanent place to live; a place of refuge. There's a longing within all of us to find home. Heaven is like home with a Father and loved ones as they're supposed to be.

How can you be sure that you'll get to that home? Is there a map or some rules to follow? No, it comes through a person — Jesus Christ Himself. As He talked about a heavenly home, He also added that He is the only way to ever truly come home.

♥   ♥   ♥

WHAT IS HEAVEN LIKE?

"And if I go and prepare a place for you, I will come again, and receive you to Myself; that where I am, there you may be also."

JESUS CHRIST
JOHN 14:3

DEATH OF COMMUNISM

Isn't it interesting that on Christmas Day, 1991, the leader of the Soviet Communist system, Mikhail Gorbechev, announced his resignation. The world watched as the red Hammer and Sickle flag was lowered for the last time. It's also interesting that the very government, which for more than 70 years tried to destroy Christianity in the Soviet Union, officially died on Christmas Day. God's sense of timing is amazing. He must have chuckled over the lowering of the Soviet flag that day, the birthday of His Son. Isn't that interesting?

My friends, God is in control of history and His plans are sure. His timing is perfect — from the birth of His Son to the end of Communism on Christmas Day. One day, in His perfect timing, Jesus will return. The way history is moving, it will not be long. Let us all be ready for His coming by walking in His will every single day.

♥   ♥   ♥

I don't know whether you've ever been invited to the White House or ever been asked to make an appearance at Buckingham Palace, but wouldn't it be amazing to have the President of the United States or the Queen of England desire to visit in your home? Even more amazing, there is a King who represents royalty and power, greater than anyone, that desires to do just that.

The Bible tells us that it's Jesus Christ, the King of Kings. He talks about our life like its a home. He says He is standing outside the door of our life. He's knocking and hoping we'll invite Him in. If you do open the door and invite Him in, He promises to enter. When He comes into your life, He brings meaning, companionship, strength and love to face the demands of life. He brings everything you need to live a complete and purposeful life.

How about it? Why not open the door today and you can have dinner with the King of Kings, forever and ever.

♥   ♥   ♥

THE INVITATION

"Behold, I stand at the door and knock; if anyone hears my voice and opens the door, I will come in to him."

JESUS CHRIST
REVELATION 3:20

One More Minute of Your Time...

Well, have you discovered that "one thing"—the answer to life? It is a personal relationship with God through Jesus Christ. In a nutshell, here is how you can have it.

BELIEVE THAT GOD LOVES YOU. He wants to have a personal relationship with you. He wants you to have a meaningful, abundant life. *(John 3:16; John 10:10b)*

THE PROBLEM = OUR SEPARATION FROM GOD. Sin separates us from God. Sin means to miss the mark. It is selfishness and a desire to do things our way rather than God's way as described in Scripture. *(Romans 6:23; James 2:10)*

THE SOLUTION = JESUS CHRIST. God has become a man in the form of His Son, Jesus, to save us from our sin. Two basic things have to be believed before we can think about becoming a Christian: 1)Jesus died for our sins, *(Romans 5:8; 6:23)* and 2)Jesus conquered sin and death by rising from the dead. *(I Corinthians 15:3-8)*

THE DECISION = TO RECEIVE CHRIST IN FAITH. It is not enough to believe who Jesus is with our minds. That's essential, but not enough. We must decide to trust Christ and receive Him by personal invitation. *(Revelation 3:20; John 1:12)*

♥   ♥   ♥

Have you done this? To learn how, turn the page…

109

*H*ow to receive Christ:

1. Admit your need. (I am a sinner.)

2. Be willing to turn from your sins. (Repent.)

3. Believe that Jesus Christ died for you on the Cross and rose from the grave.

4. Through prayer, invite Jesus Christ to come in and control your life through the Holy Spirit. (Receive Him personally as Lord and Savior.)

♥   ♥   ♥

ere is a Model of What to Pray:

Dear Lord Jesus,

I know that I am a sinner and need Your forgiveness. I believe that You died for my sins. I want to turn from my sins. I now invite You to come into my heart and life. I want to trust and follow You as Lord and Savior.

In Jesus' name. Amen.

_____   _____
Date   Signature

♥   ♥   ♥

Once You Know the "One Thing"–Then What?

This "one thing," personal faith in Christ, is the answer to a meaningful life. It's guaranteed! Once that decision is made, you want to grow in your relationship with God through Christ for the rest of your life. This can be done through:

♥ Prayer
♥ Bible study
♥ Being in church
♥ Obedience
♥ Being a witness (sharing your faith as God leads).

The best sign to know you are growing in your faith is through your love... love for God first, followed by a love for your fellow man.

May you experience this love every minute of every day. God bless you.

Bryant Wright

♥   ♥   ♥